i

The Man Who Brought Light

– ROGER SAWTELL –

An environmentally friendly book printed and bound in
England by www.printondemand-worldwide.com

This book is made entirely of chain-of-custody materials

www.fast-print.net/store.php

The Man Who Brought Light

ISBN 978-178035-061-5

First published 2011 by
FASTPRINT PUBLISHING
Peterborough, England.

THE MAN WHO BROUGHT LIGHT

The story of Edward Leslie who initiated a remarkable technical and social development in northwest Scotland

Illustrations by Colin Brash

"God was always with me then and gave me light as I walked through the darkness."
Job Chapter 29 verse 3

Preface

The idea for this story came to mind after reading Jean Giono's allegorical tale, *The Man Who Planted Trees* (1) which tells of a shepherd, Elzéard Bouffier, who planted acorns on a desolate and deserted plateau in the south of France during the middle years of the twentieth century. In due course the trees grew, the ground was stabilised, streams began to run again, the land was restored to health and people came to live there.

The story which follows describes a young engineer who developed engines to generate electricity which brought light to a mountain area and new life to the people. The illustrations by Colin Brash evoke the wild splendour of the northwest coast of Scotland.

To get the measure of a person's priorities and objectives we need to study him or her over a long period of time, decades rather than years. Elzéard Bouffier, almost alone, planted trees for thirty years. His contemporary, Edward Leslie, spent fifty years quietly developing his remote Scottish land. Their upbringing could hardly have been more different from one another but the results of their persevering work were similar, the regeneration of a beautiful landscape, tangible, long-lasting, people-centred. The world is changed for the better.

Roger Sawtell
Northampton 2011

Edward Leslie was my closest friend at university. He did not seek out my friendship as he was the most self-sufficient person imaginable, and I recollect that he did not seem to have many other friends, but as my name also began with L we were put together to carry out our 'practicals' in the engineering workshops. Together we needed to get pressure and temperature readings to demonstrate the Carnot cycle for an internal combustion engine (2), or readings to calculate the flow of water over weirs of different shapes. I was a capricious student, as much interested in people as in engines, and this was borne out by my subsequent career in management rather than research or technology, but Edward was an enthusiastic practitioner and his notes and observations were more neatly ordered than mine, so I came to rely on his work when we were writing-up our experiments and thus our friendship grew.

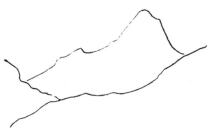

Traditional croft houses, just two rooms and a door in the middle.

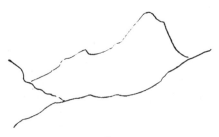

I valued it and I thought, even at that early stage, that he was destined to lead an unusual life.

We kept in touch after we graduated in the Mechanical Sciences Tripos in 1912. His mother had died giving birth to him, an only child, and he was brought up by his father, a successful accountant, in respectable but rather isolated Edinburgh society. However, soon after witnessing with pride his son's graduation as an engineer, his father died unexpectedly and Edward found himself comfortably off, almost wealthy, with no need to earn a living as his needs were modest.

Knowing his tendency to be content with his own company, I was not surprised when he wrote to tell me that he had sold the Edinburgh house and was planning to live in the 'big hoose' on an estate which his forbears had owned for generations on the far northwest coast of Scotland. To his surprise, for his father,

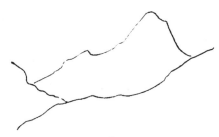

who never wanted to stray far from his desk in Edinburgh, had hardly mentioned it to him, Edward had inherited 5000 remote acres of heather and rock outcrop, and about twenty small cottages, originally provided for crofters and the estate workers, ghillies and house servants. These were traditional croft houses, just two rooms with a porch and a door in the middle(3), and they were scattered over the estate with only rough tracks leading to them. By the furthest western shore there were also another twenty such houses,which were in ruins, the walls still standing but the roofs fallen in.

I accepted his invitation to visit, to get right away from London for my annual leave. The big house had been empty for years and needed some maintenance which Edward was able to do himself as he was adept with many tools and practical trades. There was a spartan

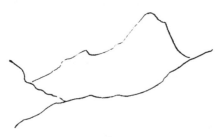

4

bedroom for me but he had closed most of the house and he lived in one huge room overlooking the sea to the west (4) One end was his kitchen and the other end his bedroom; in between he had a table, a decaying easy chair and bookshelves from floor to ceiling. An unusual habitat for the owner of a large estate but his wants seemed very simple and he did not appear to miss the trappings of the contemporary society in which I moved in London. Throughout his life he never installed a telephone and he never owned a car, which, in view of the way this story develops, was extraordinary.

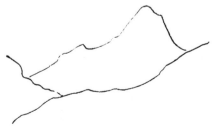

He lived in one huge room overlooking the sea.

We walked for miles among the mountains with the translucent green sea at our feet,colours not found anywhere else in our country. Often we would hardly speak for an hour and then only to decide on the route or point out a feature. Edward seemed to be at one with this terrain which had been allowed to revert to its natural state as his father had shown no interest in developing it. His boundaries were the sea to the west, a single track road to the east,the river Doran in the south and the magnificent mountain ridge of Sgurr Ban in the north. A single pole on the foreshore was sufficient to indicate his northern boundary (5).

Although Edward did not seem to need much human company, the notable exceptions were his tenants, all of whom he seemed to know well. One day on a lonely track we met Duncan who was

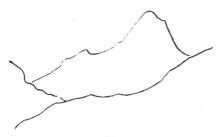

carrying an ancient shotgun which had probably belonged to his grandfather.

'Good day, Duncan,' said Edward. Duncan seemed unsure as to whether this was a greeting or a question and, after a long pause, because speech comes slowly to those who live in such places, he replied, 'Aye, good day, Mr Edward, ye'll be knowing that I'm only after the rabbits for to make a stew'.

'That's OK but please understand that I don't want my friends nor anyone else to be shooting animals just for the sport of it.'

'Aye, I know that and I have no the money for cartridges to spare. I'll mebbe trap these bunnies with a snare instead.'

Edward knew that food was scarce and he had no objection to shooting rabbits or sea fishing, by which one or two of his tenants made a precarious living, but he had no intention of allowing syndicates

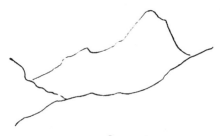

8

from the cities to shoot just for the sport of killing animals. He wanted the wildlife to develop with as little outside attention as possible. In season, there were salmon in the Doran, hares on the hills and a few red deer in the high corries. One evening we came home to find a basket of brown trout on the doorstep, caught in the small lochans by the sea. His tenants knew he was not a meat eater and if they killed a deer they kept the knowledge and the venison well out of sight.

Soon after my visit the 1914-18 war caught us both and I lost touch with him until 1919 when he again wrote inviting me to visit. I needed no persuading. We were both still young men in our twenties but rather the worse for wear.

Edward had a limp from a wound on the Somme and I was short of breath having been gassed near Ypres. Several of my university friends never returned and we were thankful to be alive. As well as

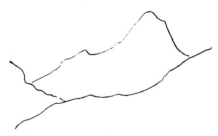

our physical disabilities we were emotionally scarred and some of our wartime memories were too horrific to dwell upon, but there were just occasional flashes of hope for a better world. For example, Edward told me he had been present at the extraordinary football match played on no-mans-land between English and German troops at Christmas 1917. Seemingly they agreed an informal temporary truce for a few hours on Christmas Day, played football and then returned each to their own trenches and continued with the 'business as usual' of trying to kill each other. Not surprisingly, this paradox stayed in his mind and showed up the tragic inhumanity of the mass slaughter in which he was unwillingly engaged. It was to affect the way he decided to spend the rest of his life.

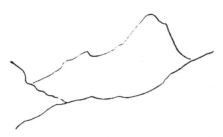

A single pole on the foreshore was sufficient to indicate his northern boundary.

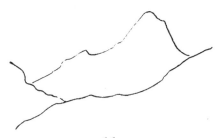

Edward seemed quieter than ever. He still walked all over the estate and hardly ever left it. He kept in touch by writing letters which young Benjie McLeod took to the post office at Kinspiel, ten miles away, where he also collected the incoming mail. Edward gave him half a crown for his twenty mile round trip and Benjie was delighted with such wealth.

'I'll be going for the post every day, Mr Edward, if you want it.'

'No, Benjie, once a week is quite sufficient and you need to get on with your schooling.'

'What with the work with the tatties and a'that there's no time for schooling in the day,' said Benjie, conveniently forgetting that he had just offered to go to Kinspiel every day, 'and then it's unco dark for the schooling wi just a candle.'

Unknown to this unwilling pupil, Edward stored this remark for he knew

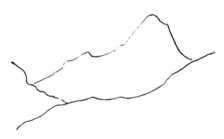

there were other children and adults who wanted to learn but were prevented by the lack of daylight. In the depth of winter it was getting dark by 3pm.

He had turned one part of his big room into a kind of chapel with a Celtic cross in the window facing the sea and a kneeling stool. I gained the impression that he spent a good deal of time in prayer and meditation although he never mentioned it to me. It was years later that I realised that his unusual lifestyle was dictated by his Christian faith and, in particular, by his understanding of Matthew's Gospel. I realise now that his practical concern for his tenants, who were even poorer than they had been before the war, was directly guided by the passage, *'inasmuch as ye have done it to one of these, my brethren, ye have done it unto me.'* (6) He never said this to me in so many words but I noticed that this verse was always on his writing

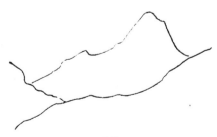

13

table, together with a quotation from a Quaker writer :-

In the topsy-turvey world of the way of God as taught by Jesus, familiar categories turn upside down: people with contagious diseases are touched and healed; a woman who prefers intellectual discussion to housework is highly valued; the unemployed get a day's wage for a few hours work; a prostitute is held up as a good example to a religious leader; the good seats at a state banquet go to the street people ... The Quaker tradition testifies that by the insight and power of the inward guide it is possible for us to live comfortably today in the upside-down world of the way of God, the reign that is both here and now and not yet. (7)

These two quotations underpinned Edward's attitude towards those living on his land and were in contrast to the

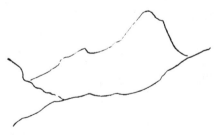

neighbouring 'sporting estates' whose wealthy owners lived elsewhere and were largely ignorant of the poverty of the local people.

He showed me his basement, another huge room which he had recently set up as a workshop with a long workbench and many tools. I was astonished to see a row of six brand-new oil engines, painted dark green with the maker's nameplate, MACLAREN, picked out in gold. They filled the floorspace and looked rather out of place in this remote spot; Edward explained with some diffidence that he was assembling them into electric generator sets for his tenants.

'Why this technology in this isolated place?', I asked. He was slow to reply and seemed lost in his own thoughts as happens to those who live most of the time alone. Eventually he said, 'I used to think that pride and greed were the dominant causes of disharmony in the

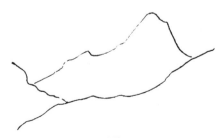

15

world and that's why we had to fight the wretched war. But I have come to realise that there is a quite different but no less hateful disharmony which is brought about by preventing our fellow men and women from developing their God-given talents. Such deprivation leads to a lack of self-esteem, then to despair and sometimes to violence. Barlinnie prison is full of capable men led to crime because of their poor image of themselves.'

'I think I follow you,' I said, 'and I know you are the least likely person to be accused of pride or greed, but what has this got to do with these engines?'

'Winter days are short in northern Scotland and if like us,' by which he meant his tenants as well as himself, 'you live on a western slope we have little daylight and even less sunlight. The day's work must be done and the oil wick lamps we use after dark are a poor help for reading or other close work. The result is

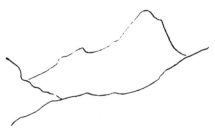

that our children are deprived of their rightful education,we are gradually being depopulated and our self-image is in decline. My plan is to provide each tenant with a generator which will produce good quality electric light. These engines are ideal. Old Maclaren is a perfectionist. He even makes his own castings in a back street in Glasgow and machines them to tolerances which other larger makers cannot match. They are small and sturdy and run at 500 rpm which is much slower and quieter than these new motor cars. The result is that they will run for years with little need of maintenance or spare parts. Just an occasional de-coke which requires a ring spanner to remove the cylinder head and an old file to scrape the carbon out of the corners. Moreover, Maclaren has developed a compact two-stage silencer with a primary and a secondary box so that the engine is amazingly quiet and not intrusive, housed

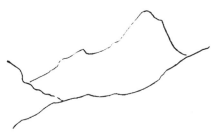

in a shed or even a cave behind the house.'

Edward seldom made such a long speech and I could see that his plan was the result of much thought about the condition of men and women recovering from the appalling disharmonies of the war. I learned that 'old Maclaren' was a Scottish engineer who, as a young man had worked for Crossley Bros. Ltd. near Manchester, leading manufacturers of gas and oil engines which they exported all over the world. In their advertising they claimed to have supplied over a hundred thousand engines and had circumvented the German patents for diesels by developing a two-stroke design in which there was a power stroke for every revolution of the crankshaft. This made their engines smoother and quieter than the four-stroke diesels developed in Germany.

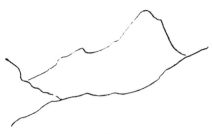

Maclaren worked on this development for years at Crossleys, always believing that he could improve the design if only he had the chance to build his own engines, unrestrained by the conservative Crossley philosophy.

'Nay, lad,' said his boss, 'stay with what you know about and let others take the risk. Crossleys would die if we got it wrong.'

But Maclaren was unconvinced and only too eager to take a risk if only he had the money. Then he had a once-in-a-lifetime chance when his uncle died and left him enough money to set up his own small engineering business in Glasgow. For nearly two years Maclaren Ltd. produced nothing to sell but he worked all hours, first on the drawing board and then in the workshop,building the first production engine in 1920. His design was simpler and even more reliable than the Crossleys and it had the important feature

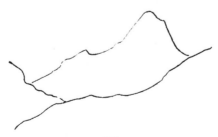

that it would run on relatively unrefined fuel (8) Years of thought and countless hours of workshop time paid-off with this rugged design which then remained in production for over thirty years. But seeing these first engines delivered to Edward's place in 1923, the obvious thought occurred to me that the cost of diesel oil and the difficulty of transporting it to northwest Scotland must make them uneconomic except for wealthy lairds.

'Well, yes,' said Edward, 'but this is where I consider I may have made a breakthrough. I have been experimenting with different fuels.....'

'How about fish oil,' I said, 'there are millions of herrings out there?'

'We tried that but it did not combust satisfactorily in the Maclarens and the smell was atrocious. We also tried rape seed oil but rape won't grow round here, too cold. Then I discovered that shale oil was being produced in Scotland by

heating the bitumen in shale, a soft laminated rock found near coal deposits. It worked! It is possible to inject this oil directly into the cylinder in the fine spray needed for it to ignite under pressure. No spark required. It's called compression ignition, diesel technology.'

However, the cost of buying this shale oil from the Scottish coalfields in Lanarkshire still made it uneconomic for Edward's purposes and he was disconsolate. Then, when none of his experiments seemed to be showing promise he told me of a conversation with Benjie, who regularly visited Edward's workshop to deliver his post.

' There's a terrible smell in here, Mr Edward,' said Benjie, 'and I ken it's like what comes off that stack of stanes by the new drift mine in Kinspiel.'

' What kind of stones are you talking about, Benjie?'

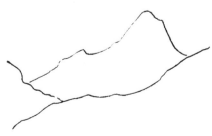

' It's what they pull out of the mine to get to the coal. My cousin, Jamie, works there. Do you want me to fetch a load on the ponies next time I go for the post.' There was a glint in Benjie's eye as he envisaged many more half-crowns coming his way.

Sure enough, the Kinspiel drift mine, recently opened by a handful of enterprising men to escape from Glasgow, was shipping coal to the south but the shale was just piling up as a slag heap by the mine. So the following week Benjie took the two ponies, Bill and Ben, and filled the panniers with shale, and walked them back to Edward's workshop.

' The mine man wudna take ony money,' said Benjie, 'for he was happy to get the stuff out o' his yard. Mebbe I'll tak him a few herrings next week and he'll be fine.'

The shale was so oily that Edward had the idea that the oil might be extracted

with a centrifuge, a heavy duty version of the domestic spin dryer, and after weeks of trials with different speeds and temperatures, he suceeded, without the need of expensive distillation plant, in producing an oil which worked well in the Maclarens. Thereafter, hardly a week went by without Benjie carrying a letter about the design of fuel injectors to 'old Mac' in Glasgow and returning with a load of shale. The workshop became the smallest and cleanest oil producer imaginable and Edward was happy again. Mac replied with meticulous drawings of the modifications he needed to make to the fuel injectors.

They were two of a kind, Edward and Mac, men who were happier tinkering with engines than talking to people, both brilliant engineers capable of making fine quality components with simple machine tools. Edward used a doctor's stethoscope to listen to the valve mechanism on the

Maclarens, like a doctor listening to his patient's chest. A good analogy because both of them had the same kind of understanding and sympathy with engines that a good doctor has with his patients. Love is not too strong a word to describe their relationship with the Maclarens and the engines had been made 'with love' by Mac. Surprisingly, they never met but their voluminous correspondence was the basis for a friendship which lasted thirty years. Edward bequeathed the papers to me and I have kept them carefully as a record of an engineering development which brought fulfilment to many people. Some day a Ph.D student might want to write it up.

Mac never wanted his business to grow to more than a handful of reliable men, mostly veterans who had trained in the Clyde shipyards before the 1914-18 war. Their output of four engines per week was

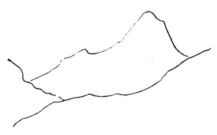

invariably sold months in advance but when his accountant told him he had enough accumulated capital to increase production, Mac declined. ' Four good engines, tuned and tested by four good craftsmen are more important to me than forty engines made on a production line.' he said. Although Mac was the sole owner, most of the decisions were made by everyone sitting round a large table in one corner of the Glasgow workshop, at tea break. They resisted all attempts to buy them out. Mac was ten years older than Edward and he died in 1952, aged 71. Working alone late at night, finishing one of the engines due to be despatched to Edward, he had a heart attack and was found the following morning, slumped over the engine, seeming to be holding it in a loving embrace. The business died with him because his small band of employees did not have the heart to continue. They finished the work in progress, delivered the last engines to

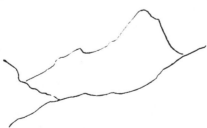

Edward and locked the doors. The premises were sold to the adjoining grocery shop which pulled down the buildings and used the site to make a car park. Later it became a supermarket and later still I had a commemorative plaque cast and asked them to mount it on the outside wall where it still remains:

On this site Maclaren oil engines were manufactured between 1921 and 1952, bringing light and new life to many people in Scotland

Perhaps the business would have died anyway because by the 1950's mains power was becoming more widely available even in the far northwest and demand for the Maclarens would have diminished. However, Mac's legacy, and he would have asked no other, was two thousand engines quietly chugging away in remote places, unnoticed by tourists but producing precious light and enabling learning for

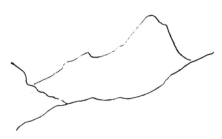

many who would otherwise not have had the opportunity.

Back in the 1920's, on my next visit, Edward's house and his routine were unchanged. Ten houses had been running generators for some years and the results were beginning to show. Two boys had done well enough at school to go to college in Glasgow and one had returned to find 'the mac' still running sweetly in the back hut. Due to 'the electric', a group of feisty women had been able to knit many more heavy wool jerseys and, with Edward's help, were registering as an employee-owned business, Doran Co-operative Ltd., to sell them to the fishing fleets based at Lochinver and Kinlochbervie. I was impressed and it became my habit to visit Edward every summer, to walk about the wild country and discuss the developments. He had no other visitors as far as I knew, so the changes he was making on the estate were hardly known

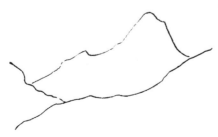

outside the locality. As the young people came back from college, enterprise returned to the area. One bought a van to make a weekly provisioning trip to Inverness for the tenants, and several now had building skills. Every year one or more of the ruined croft houses was rebuilt, new people came and the school had to be re-opened after thirty years closure.

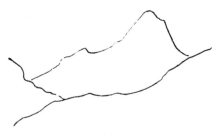

Always happy for walkers to cross his territory.

Edward had always been happy for walkers to cross his territory (9). Some would ask permission at the big house, others, walking up the coast to Cape Wrath would not realise they were on the estate because he never had signs erected. It was not difficult to wade across the Doran except when it was in flood in the not uncommon rainy seasons. Edward decided to designate a rebuilt croft house, on the shoreline, as a bothy for anyone to stay overnight.

The only facilities were a stack of dry wood, a fireplace and a wooden sleeping platform. The door was never locked and the notice on it said simply, ' Doran Bothy. There is good water in the burn. Please leave this place as you find it'.

The visitor's book has some interesting entries:-

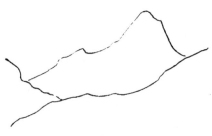

' Thanks for a dry night – next stop Cape Wrath'

' Dry night my foot. We've been on the red wine since it got dark and now I think I can see the sunrise but maybe it's an alcoholic illusion. There are sufficient empties to keep the bothy in candle holders for years to come.'

' Saw two sea otters down on the shore - wonderful.'

' We had a grand craic. Some said the rain was horizontal, others argued that it was vertical.'

' Will the sinner that took the wood-splitting axe please return it.'

Only once, Edward told me, was unfair advantage taken of the bothy. A group of unemployed shipyard workers from Glasgow stayed for at least a week, left it in a mess, broke one of the roof sheets and did not replace the firewood stack. Some landlords would have closed it down

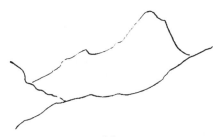

but Edward said he was aware of the despair of longterm unemployment and he did not hold them to account. All this was in the 1930's, so he was a pioneer of bothies long before there was any organisation to help *'to maintain simple shelters in remote country'* but, as one who loved wild and lonely places, he lived long enough to become a member of the Mountain Bothies Association when it was founded in 1965 (10)

After I had spent a holiday on a Greek island which was isolated and mountainous, not unlike Scotland but much warmer, I suggested to Edward that he might get a donkey or two but he decided that donkeys would not withstand the dark and damp of north Scotland. So the two sturdy ponies were the standard freight carriers for years (11). Benjie, like Edward, seldom left Doran and lived in one of the rebuilt croft houses as long as I can remember. He delivered the shale oil

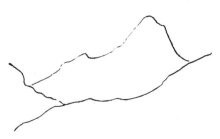

to each house in five-gallon cans counterbalanced across the ponies' backs. I had seen donkeys carrying water in this manner in Greece and it was a strange parallel to observe the ponies, in single file on a skyline beyond Edward's house, plodding patiently westwards towards the furthest croft houses near the sea.

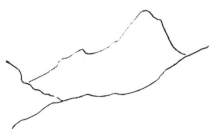

Two ponies were the standard freight carriers

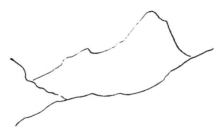

In thinking out what to do with the land, Edward's dilemma was that he loved solitude and needed little company but yet he was deeply concerned to broaden the lives of others rather than keep the estate to himself. He wanted to provide ways for the tenants to earn a living and stem the depopulation of the far west coast. He believed that material poverty and deprivation often led to clinical depression and also to spiritual poverty, so that many were doubly impoverished. He spent many hours dwelling on this matter and looking for the appropriate way forward, having decided that he should make it more possible for visitors to come to Doran. Although I saw him as a recluse, he was not a detached dreamer but an intensely practical man always looking for ways to use limited resources, be it light from the sun as the source of all energy or light from that spiritual source we call God. I was aware of his generosity of time, place and money but the solution he arrived at,

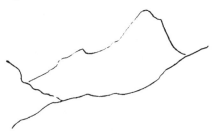

slowly and steadily in the turmoil of the 1930's, surprised me by its novelty and vision.

Using his drawing board he made working drawings for the restoration of two adjacent croft house to be an adventure centre, one house to be a bunkhouse with showers and a drying room and the other to be a living room with a huge west window, comfortable chairs and a well-equipped kitchen. An open passageway with a turf roof joined the two and acted as a store for peat and equipment. The result was an attractive building, appropriate to the terrain, with a superb view to seaward. Power was provided by two Maclarens installed in a nearby cave; their exhaust system together with a double-insulated wooden doorway fitted to the mouth of the cave rendered them soundproof from the houses. He contracted some of the tenants, who had now become an

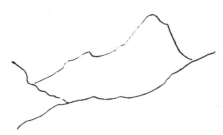

experienced group of building craftsmen, to carry out the restoration which took them about a year. He asked two young men, Alex and Jake, to train as leaders of outdoor activities and they took the courses required for good practice and safety on land and sea. With some diffidence, he asked me to act as a kind of informal agent in London and I was pleased to respond as a way to return his hospitality because there was no way he would have enjoyed staying in my rather noisy London flat. My task was to write, phone and visit the headteachers of London secondary schools, to invite them to organise holiday groups to spend a week at Doran. We called it Doran Adventure and made it as clear as possible that it was a week of outdoor adventure and indoor discussion. The latter was Edward's contribution; he made no claim to be a teacher or charismatic preacher but he talked about the things which were important to him, the ever-

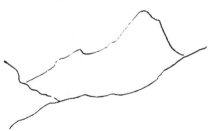

changing colours of the sea and sky, the beauty of the hills. He linked this with God as creator - how else can you explain a west highland sunset? - and Jesus as the example to follow.

I thought, me of little faith, that this strange mixture, physical and spiritual, might be a recipe for failure. Those attracted by the challenges of the hills and the sea would resent the faith component, and those attracted by the spiritual might not choose to be challenged by the outdoors. I was wrong. Many of the boys who came to Doran Adventure, of all abilities and disabilities, warmed to Edward's quiet approach to these matters because they detected something intrinsically 'good' about him. He was not pious in the accepted sense of the word, nor authoritarian, and he seemed to be content to be as much a servant as a leader, as much a doer as an intellectual, a generous spirit, a man for others. They

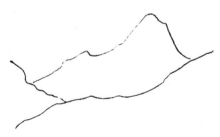

did not often put such thoughts into words but, as an occasional visitor to the summer courses, I could detect it. There was also hard evidence because some returned to live and work at Doran, at least two became ordained ministers and others trained as youth leaders. Some travelled thousands of miles to be present and give thanks at the memorial service after Edward died, in 1973.

In the 1930's Doran Advenure did not develop quickly. It was a time of serious economic depression and we knew that many of the boys from impoverished east end families were unlikely to go away anywhere during the school holidays. Edward kept the cost low and fuel was almost the only direct expense because the groups brought their own food with them. We had a bursary fund to help boys whose parents could not afford to pay. Nevertheless the take-up was slow and despite my publicity efforts in London,it

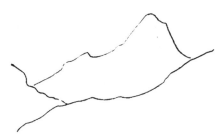

was ten years before the summer weeks were fully booked, and then came the 1939-45 war. But Edward was not in a hurry and Doran Adventure was up and running again by 1950. Later, when similar organisations like Outward Bound were initiated, Doran was well established and the courses had to be booked a year ahead. They were always full.

The boys themselves did all the chores and this in itself was a new experience because most of them came from homes where it was taken for granted that women did all the household work. I overheard a remark,

'You'll have to show us how to do this washing up, Jake, my ma never lets us near the sink. She says we'll break all her precious pots.' Jake and Alex organised the daily activities of exploring, hill walking, and swimming for the hardy at a small sandy beach near the centre. The abundant wildlife was observed; few of the

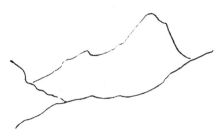

boys had ever seen a buzzard or a red deer and I don't suppose any had seen a sea-otter of which there were quite a number along the shoreline.

The week culminated with a full day expedition which included the ascent of Sgurr Ban as part of a circuit of ten miles walking over trackless heather and rock outcrop. An optional short cut was possible by swimming 400 yards across the sea loch instead of the three mile walk round the head of the loch. Edward had designed a double-thickness waterproof sack which boots and clothes could be put into for this crossing. The sack, with built-in flotation, was then attached to a harness and towed behind the swimmer. This option, not surprisingly, was taken-up by only a few as the water never warms up much on that coast.

' Are you going to do the swim, Bob, or walk round the top?'

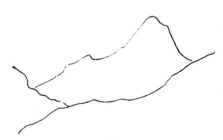

' Me, swim? It 'ud freeze me balls off. I'd walk ten miles to avoid it, let alone three.'

There was no competitive element in this very demanding expedition. The achievement was for each boy as an individual and often it was the seemingly least able who gained most from completing the circuit.

The Doran Co-operative, the women's work project, made the buoyancy bags for Doran Adventure and tried selling them to the fishermen at Lochinver and Kinlochbervie along with the knitted sweaters, but without much success as few of the fishermen could swim and trusted to providence rather than flotation bags if they were washed overboard.

In the evenings Edward would walk down for the discussion, sometimes bringing a basket of mackerel or some home-baked bread. I was with him on one such evening when a bright cockney boy said:

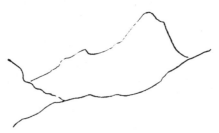

'Mr Edward, with all this land you could build a big hotel and get some of them rich London folk here.'

Edward said, 'That's not what I want to do. They can look after themselves.

I want to give boys like you the opportunity to see something different from London.'

' OK but I think I'd be lonely here with no hustle and bustle and how can you "do unto others" if there are hardly any others to do unto?'

'Good question. I think the answer is that some doing unto others is maintaining quiet places for people to come to, to enable them to regain energy for the hustle.'

'Yea, but I still think I'd be lonely if it wasn't for my mates here with me.'

What about the Maclarens? The 1939-45 war came and went and they kept on

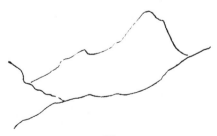

43

generating light. Usually an hour a day was sufficient to keep the batteries fully charged and this added at least four hours a day to the time available for work in the house or studying or reading. Edward, now in his fifties, continued his placid lifestyle. In order to retain the concept of a community helping each other, he did not sell any of the houses nor did he have any hesitation in declining requests from wealthy Americans or other deerstalkers to rent the estate for the summer months. He still knew all the residents, both the ageing original tenants and the newcomers. He said little about them to me but it was impossible for him to conceal that he was aware of their strengths and occasional weaknesses, their opportunities and their tribulations, and he loved them all. He asked for no other company so very few people outside the area knew anything of Doran and I was privileged to be his annual guest.

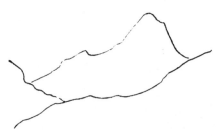

The last time I saw him was in 1972. He was rather frail but remained living in his house with willing help from the tenants. He called them community members and there were now nearly forty houses occupied and over a hundred people, including lots of children. They had opened a community shop and post office and the Forestry Commission had awarded them a contract to plant trees on the most barren part of the estate. Edward's living room was still just large enough for the monthly community meetings and a church service on Sundays. The members regarded him less as a landlord and more as a mentor and wise friend. Unable to walk much he sat for hours at the west window, contemplating the incomparable view which had inspired him for over half a century. Some of the Maclarens were still running but mains electricity, at last, was reaching out to these farthest places so most of the engines, some nearly fifty

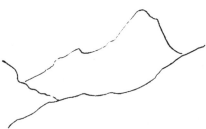

years old, were honourably retired. At least one is in a Scottish museum, because I took it there with an explanatory notice.

Edward was never directly engaged in politics, that would not have been his style at all. But if social democracy can be defined as a determination to change the conditions which lead to suffering, such as material poverty, lack of education, dull work, then he was undoubtedly a social democrat, a political person. He saw his life at Doran as a contribution to the Kingdom, that blending of the spiritual and material worlds described in the four Gospels, *'your kingdom come on earth as it is in heaven'.*

He died peacefully at Raigmore Hospital, Inverness, on 18 September 1973, aged 82. I was happy to declaim this prayer at his funeral:-

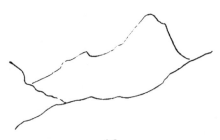

46

Heavenly Father, we thank you for those we love but see no longer. As we remember Edward and give thanks for his life, hold before us our beginning and our ending, the dust from which we come and the death to which we move, in the sure and certain hope of resurrection and the coming of the Kingdom, on earth as in heaven.

Edward brought light in more ways than one. A life well lived.

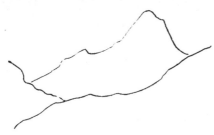

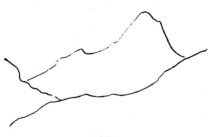

NOTES

(1) *The Man Who Planted Trees* by Jean Giono (Harvill Press 1996)

(2) Carnot cycle: *an idealised reversible heat-engine cycle giving maximum efficiency* (Collins English Dictionary)

(3) see drawing of croft house

(4) see drawing of Edward's room

(5) see drawing of pole on shore

(6) The bible quotation is from Matthews Gospel chapter 25 verse 40 (Authorised Version)

(7) The Quaker quotation is by Ursula Jane O'Shea from her Backhouse Lecture *Living the Way*

(8) Because these engines are slow-running, there is more time for the fuel to ignite in the cylinder, compared to a car engine. Thus it is

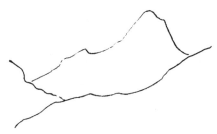

possible to have a lower compression ratio and use less-refined fuel than cars.

(9)   See drawing of walkers

(10) Mountain   Bothies   Association
www.mountainbothies.org.uk

(11) See drawing of ponies

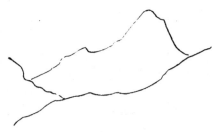